books

BO

www.booksbyboxer.com

Published in the UK by
Books By Boxer, Leeds, LS13 4BS
© 2020 SILVEY-JEX PARTNERSHIP
All Rights Reserved
Printed In China

ISBN: 9781909732568

IF THERE WERE ELEVEN ELVES
AND ANOTHER ONE CAME ALONG,
WHAT WOULD HE BE?

THE TWELF!

WHAT DO ELVES SING
TO SANTA?

'FREEZE A JOLLY GOOD FELLOW'

WHAT DO YOU CALL
AN ELF WALKING
BACKWARDS ?

A FLE!

WHAT DO SNOWMEN EAT FOR
BREAKFAST

ICE CRISPIES!

HOW LONG SHOULD AN
ELF'S LEGS BE ?

JUST LONG ENOUGH TO
REACH THE GROUND!

IF ATHLETES GET ATHLETE'S
FOOT, WHAT DO ELVES GET?

MISTLE-TOES!

WHAT KIND OF MOTORCYCLE
DOES SANTA RIDE?

A HOLLY DAVIDSON

WHAT DO YOU GET WHEN YOU
CROSS A DUCK WITH SANTA?

A CHRISTMAS QUACKER

WHAT IS A FEMALE ELF CALLED?

A SHELF!

WHERE DO YOU FIND ELVES?

DEPENDS WHERE YOU LEFT THEM!

WHAT DO SANTA'S ELVES
DO AFTER SCHOOL?

THEIR GNOMEWORK!

WHO SINGS 'BLUE CHRISTMAS'
AND MAKES TOY GUITARS?

ELFIS!

WHY DID SANTA TELL
ONE OF HIS ELVES OFF?

BECAUSE HE WAS
'GOBLIN' HIS DINNER!

WHAT KIND OF BREAD DO ELVES MAKE SANDWICHES WITH?

SHORTBREAD OF COURSE!

WHAT KIND OF MONEY DO ELVES USE?

JINGLE BILLS!

WHAT DID THE ELF SAY
WAS THE FIRST STEP IN
USING A CHRISTMAS COMPUTER?

"FIRST, YULE LOGON"!

WHAT HAPPENS TO NAUGHTY ELVES?

THEY GET THE SACK!

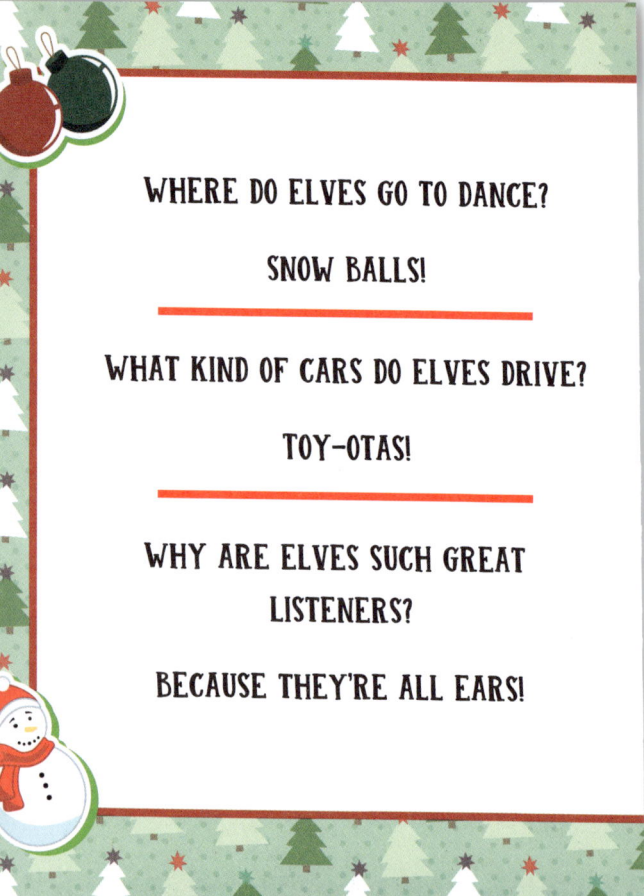

WHERE DO ELVES GO TO DANCE?

SNOW BALLS!

WHAT KIND OF CARS DO ELVES DRIVE?

TOY-OTAS!

WHY ARE ELVES SUCH GREAT LISTENERS?

BECAUSE THEY'RE ALL EARS!

ONE ELF SAID TO ANOTHER ELF,
"WE HAD GRANDMA FOR CHRISTMAS DINNER".
AND THE OTHER ELF SAID,

"REALLY? WE HAD TURKEY!"

WHAT DO YOU CALL AN ELF
THAT WON THE LOTTERY?

WELFY!

WHY DID THE ELVES SPELL
CHRISTMAS N-O-E?

BECAUSE SANTA HAD SAID, "NO L!"

WHAT KIND OF PHOTOGRAPHS
DO ELVES LIKE TO TAKE?

ELFIES!

WHERE DO SANTA'S HELPERS
GO WHEN THEY'RE POORLY?

THE ELF CENTRE!

WHAT IS GREEN, WHITE AND
RED ALL OVER?

A SUNBURNED ELF!

WHAT SONG DID THE ELVES SING
AT THE SNOWMAN'S BIRTHDAY PARTY?

FREEZE A JOLLY GOOD FELLOW!

WHAT DO YOU CALL AN ELF
WEARING EAR MUFFS?

ANYTHING YOU WANT.
HE CAN'T HEAR YOU!

WHAT DO YOU CALL AN ELF THAT
HELPS HIS ELEVEN FRIENDS?

THE TWELF!

WHAT DOES MRS CLAUS USE TO
MAKE A CHRISTMAS CAKE?

ELF-RAISING FLOUR!

WHAT DO YOU CALL A FROZEN ELF HANGING FROM THE CEILING?

AN ELFCICLE!

HOW DID THE REINDEER LEARN TO PLAY PIANO?

HE WAS ELF-TAUGHT.

WHAT DO YOU CALL AN ELF WHO
TELLS SILLY CHRISTMAS JOKES?

A REAL CHRISTMAS CARD!

WHY DID THE ELVES ASK THE
TURKEY TO JOIN THE BAND?

BECAUSE HE HAD
THE DRUM STICKS!

WHERE DOES SANTA GET HIS HELPERS?

FROM THE NATIONAL ELF SERVICE!

WHAT DO YOU CALL SANTA'S SINGING ELVES?

WRAPPERS!

WHAT DO THE ELVES COOK WITH
IN THE KITCHEN?

A UTINSEL.

WHY ARE SANTA'S ELVES
SOMETIMES CALLED EVES?

AT CHRISTMAS, THERE IS NOEL.

WHAT ARE ELVES GOOD AT
RUNNING?

SMALL BUSINESSES.

WHY DON'T ELVES READ
LONG BOOKS?

THEY LIKE SHORT
STORIES BETTER!

SANTA RIDES IN A SLEIGH.
WHAT DO ELVES RIDE IN?

MINIVANS!.

WHY DID SANTA'S HELPER WANT
TO KEEP THE PRESENTS TO HIMSELF?

BECAUSE HE WAS A BIT ELFISH.

WHAT'S THE DIFFERENCE BETWEEN
CARDI B AND AN ELF?

AN ELF CAN WRAP.

YOU GUYS, I JUST DREW A REALLY COOL CREATURE. IT'S HALF MOOSE, HALF ELF!

SORRY TO BOAST, I'M JUST FEELING PRETTY PROUD OF MOOSE-ELF.

WHY DO YOU NEVER SEE
FATHER CHRISTMAS IN HOSPITAL?

HE HAS PRIVATE ELF CARE.

WHY DO ELVES MAKE
GREAT HOUSE GUESTS?

THEY ONLY STAY
FOR A SHORT TIME!

DID YOU KNOW THAT SANTA'S NOT
ALLOWED TO GO DOWN CHIMNEYS
NEXT YEAR?

IT WAS DECLARED UNSAFE BY
THE ELF AND SAFETY COMMISSION.

WHAT TYPE OF ELF HAS
THE MOST BOOKS?

A BOOKSHELF.

WHAT DID THE ELF GET WHEN
HE CROSSED A BELL WITH A SKUNK?
JINGLE SMELLS.

WHY DO ALL ELVES LOOK ALIKE?

BECAUSE THERE IS LITTLE
DIFFERENCE BETWEEN THEM!

WHEN WILL THE ELF ARRIVE?

SHORTLY!

WHAT DO ELVES DO ON HOLIDAYS?

TAKE SHORT VACATIONS!

WHY DID THE ELF FLUNK
OUT OF SCHOOL?

HE HAD A SHORT ATTENTION SPAN!

WHY WAS THE ELVES
SLED REPOSSESSED?

HE WAS A LITTLE BEHIND
ON HIS PAYMENTS!

WHY DO ELVES MAKE
TERRIBLE STOCKBROKERS?

THEY ALWAYS WANT
TO SELL SHORT!

WHY COULDN'T THE ELF
PAY RENT?

HE WAS A LITTLE SHORT
THIS MONTH!

I WISH I COULD AFFORD RUDOLPH
AND BLITZEN DECORATIONS FOR
MY TREE THIS YEAR.

UNFORTUNATELY, THEY'RE TWO DEER.

WHAT DO SNOWMEN HAVE FOR BREAKFAST?

FROSTIES!

AN ELF AND A FISH WALK INTO A BAR.

THE FISH SAYS TO THE ELF "YOU KNOW WHAT,
WE SHOULD CREATE A LANGUAGE".

THE ELF RESPONDS
"SURE, WHAT SHOULD WE CALL IT?"

"ELFISH"

WHAT IS A SKUNKS FAVORITE CHRISTMAS SONG?

JINGLE SMELLS!

HOW DOES DARTH VADER ENJOY HIS CHRISTMAS TURKEY?

ON THE DARK SIDE!

WHEN IS A CHRISTMAS DINNER
BAD FOR YOUR HEALTH?

WHEN YOU'RE THE TURKEY...

WHAT DO SNOWMEN EAT
FOR LUNCH?

ICEBURGERS!

SISTER: WHAT ARE YOU GIVING
MOM AND DAD FOR CHRISTMAS?

BROTHER: A LIST OF
EVERYTHING I WANT!

JOE: WHAT NATIONALITY IS SANTA CLAUS

MOE: WHAT?

JOE: NORTH POLISH.

WHO LIVES AT THE NORTH POLE, MAKES TOYS AND RIDES AROUND IN A PUMPKIN?

CINDER-ELF-A!

HOW MANY ELVES DOES IT TAKE TO CHANGE A LIGHT BULB?

TEN! ONE TO CHANGE THE LIGHT BULB AND NINE TO STAND ON EACH OTHER'S SHOULDERS!

WHERE DOES SANTA STAY
WHEN HE IS ON HOLIDAY?

AT A HO-HO-HOTEL..

WHAT DO YOU CALL FROSTY
THE SNOWMAN IN MAY?

A PUDDLE!

WHAT DID THE SNOWMAN
SAY TO THE ROBIN?

I HAVE SNOW IDEA!

WHY DOES SANTA WORK
AT THE NORTH POLE?

BECAUSE THE PENGUINS KICKED
HIM OUT OF THE SOUTH POLE!

KNOCK KNOCK.
WHO'S THERE?
MARY.
MARY WHO?
MERRY CHRISTMAS.

WHAT DO YOU CALL
A BLIND REINDEER?

NO IDEA

WHAT DID THE KREMLIN SEND
MI6 IN THEIR CHRISTMAS HAMPER?

A MINCE SPY.

WHAT FALLS AT THE NORTH
POLE BUT NEVER GETS HURT?

SNOW.

WHAT DID THE DRUNK SNOWMAN
SAY TO THE CARROT?

GET OUT OF MY FACE!

WHAT'S AN ELVES FAVOURITE
FOOD?

MISTLE-TOAST!

WHY WAS THE TURKEY NOT HUNGRY AT THE CHRISTMAS PARTY?

HE WAS ALREADY STUFFED!

WHICH OF SANTA'S REINDEER HAS BAD MANNERS?

RUDE-OLPH

WHY COULDN'T THE SKELETON GO TO THE CHRISTMAS PARTY?

HE HAD NO-BODY TO GO WITH

WHAT HAPPEND TO THE MAN WHO STOLE AN ADVENT CALENDER?

HE GOT 24 DAYS!

HOW DOES SANTA KEEP TRACK OF ALL THE FIREPLACES HE'S VISITED?

HE KEEPS A LOG BOOK.

WHAT HAPPENED WHEN SANTA GOT STUCK IN THE CHIMNEY?

HE HAD AN ATTACK OF CLAUSTROPHOBIA.

WHY WAS THE SNOWMAN LOOKING
THROUGH THE CARROTS?

HE WAS PICKING HIS NOSE!

WHAT DOES SANTA DO WITH FAT ELVES?

HE SENDS THEM TO AN ELF FARM!

WHAT IS THE BEST CHRISTMAS PRESENT?

A BROKEN DRUM, YOU CAN'T BEAT IT!

ACCORDING TO MY KIDS' CHRISTMAS LISTS,
THEY THINK THIS PARENTING
GIG PAYS PRETTY WELL.

WHY IS CHRISTMAS JUST
LIKE A DAY AT THE OFFICE?

YOU DO ALL THE WORK AND
THE FAT GUY WITH THE SUIT
GETS ALL THE CREDIT.

WHAT DO YOU CALL AN ELF WHO RUNS OFF AND STOPS WORKING FOR SANTA?

A REBEL WITHOUT A CLAUS!

WHAT IS THE TECHNICAL NAME FOR SANTA'S ELVES?

SUBORDINATE CLAUSES.

WHAT DID THE SNOWMAN SAY TO THE ELF?

CAN YOU SMELL CARROTS?

HOW DO ELVES GET TO WORK?

BY ICICLE!

WHY WAS THE ELF SO ANGRY?

HE ONLY HAD A SHORT FUSE!.

FUN IS OUR BUSINESS

www.boxergifts.com